BAD
HABITS

Library and Archives Canada Cataloguing in Publication

Title: Bad habits / by Fraser Sutherland.

Names: Sutherland, Fraser, author.

Description: Poems.

Identifiers: Canadiana (print) 20190075627 | Canadiana (ebook) 20190075651 | ISBN 9781771613453 (softcover) | ISBN 9781771613460 (HTML) | ISBN 9781771613477 (Kindle)

Classification: LCC PS8587.U79 B33 2019 | DDC C811/.54—dc23

Published by Mosaic Press, Oakville, Ontario, Canada, 2019.

MOSAIC PRESS, Publishers
Copyright © Fraser Sutherland, 2019

Cover image "Study of Three Skulls" [detail] (Unknown maker) courtesy of the Getty's Open Content Program

ONTARIO ARTS COUNCIL
CONSEIL DES ARTS DE L'ONTARIO
an Ontario government agency
un organisme du gouvernement de l'Ontario

We acknowledge the Ontario Arts Council
for their support of our publishing program

Funded by the Government of Canada
Financé par le gouvernement du Canada

MOSAIC PRESS
1252 Speers Road, Units 1 & 2
Oakville, Ontario L6L 5N9
phone: (905) 825-2130

info@mosaic-press.com

BAD
HABITS

Fraser Sutherland

In Memory of

Alison Sutherland

1946-2018

TABLE OF CONTENTS

ACKNOWLEDGEMENTS

None of the poems here have appeared in previous collections. Some have been published in print or online, occasionally in a slightly different form, in *The Communicator, Draft, The Idler, The Maynard, This Magazine,* and *Trust the Dawning Future S'Ouvrir au Monde à Venir* (Canada), *ZiN Daily* (Croatia), *Stavaranj* (Serbia), *Sentinel Literary Quarterly* (United Kingdom), *Carcinogenic Poetry, Carnival Magazine, Grey Sparrow Journal,* and *Loch Raven Review* (United States).

AN INTRODUCTION TO
FRASER SUTHERLAND

"Working in various literary genres has had a peculiar effect on me. As soon as I've started working in one genre, I start feeling guilty about not doing something else."

"Poetry can't defeat ongoing ignorance, repetitive wrong-doing, physical deterioration nor persona extinction. But to say a few meaningful words about being in the world in the face of infinity and eternity – well, that's something."

"I'm...curmudgeon, contrarian, realist by turns; but basically? I'm a counterpuncher."

"Canadian poetry also faces structural problems. An unending series of arts-council subsidized first books drop off the production line into a void. Few receive reviews; and, those that do receive them are usually superficial or sycophantic. Even more regrettably, no one attempts an overview of the poet's working past, much less our collective literary past. The same is true of publishing...Publicity replaces criticism while big cash prizes become Potemkin-Village substitutes for a healthy engaged culture."

"One apparent oddity on my CV, by no means the only one, is my work on dictionaries. For many years I earned a minimum-wage living as a freelance, self-taught lexicographer, chiefly dealing with definitions. Apart from some cross-over with creative work, editing and writing definitions has had its obsessive-compulsive satisfactions."

"It's just as hard as ever to be a writer; to make something fresh, something good. And it's just as hard as ever to find wisdom."

"The idea of poetry-writing as therapy is especially seductive; if you're writing a poem and it's going well there's no better feeling in the world."

"Geographically, I'm a displaced, unreconstructed Nova Scotian farm boy. I kept returning home through adulthood, only to find I wasn't at home. But I'm a Maritimer, and always will be. Given a Scottish-Canadian background, one was expected to get an education and make good. Instead, I slowly, systematically set about making myself unemployable."

"Somehow, a good writer has to work aslant to the existing order. For a writer to be popular, to win prizes, to be feted by the media – those to me are grounds for suspicion. If the trappings of public success, however welcome, began to descend on me I'd start to suspect myself."

"Existentially, I think writers have to be moved by a certain dissatisfaction with the way things are. Even a poem in praise of life and the living implies that it's necessary to add something to the sum of the world, that a step is being taken toward redemption and completion."

Fraser Sutherland
Toronto. ON

I. BAD HABITS

Bad Habits

Bad habits silt
and from the ooze bubbles rise.
Here's one: distress. Prick it.
Another surfaces: discomfort.
One more: pain.

The air is filled with the sound of tiny pops,
bad habits. This cesspit was the time you spent,
each habit an increment.

Plunge your hand. It sticks like tar
from a million drags, the stink of drinks,
a burp from the second helping.

You are paying for it,
say the Pharisees and Sadducees,
secure on their plinths.

Now you must look down into your septic tank,
you must raise your eyes to their sepulchres,
and you must choose.

Diagnosis

You feel fine.
You go to the doctor.
The doctor gives you the results.
"It's not good."

You feel fine.
You go to the doctor.
He tells you after the surgery,
"The prognosis is slightly negative."

You feel fine.
You go to the doctor.
He looks at the chart.
"I'm afraid it's worse."

You feel fine.
You go to the doctor.
He shakes his head,.
"Sorry, you don't have long to live."

You fall dead at his feet.

Pills

Sure, they can relieve a muscle cramp,
quiet a headache, stop marauding infections,
give a semblance of a good night's sleep.
But what of pills taken decade after decade?
They don't prevent fits of fury,
meltdowns of misery, the griefs of loss.
We don't know if all might be worse
without them. We don't know.
Some things have no cure, it seems.
But we keep taking the pills,
in faith, as a habit, one after one.

II. PROGENITORS

Ash & Dottle

I am sitting in a Muskoka chair on a dock
over a drinkable northern Ontario lake, smoking a pipe,
admiring the trees admire themselves in water,
watching arrowhead wakes of speedboat waterbugs.
I am thinking of my father in his window chair.
He's also smoking a pipe,
the blackened bowl cradled in his paw
burned down to gurgle, juice, and dottle,
comfort, warmth, and foulness.
Smoke and stillness surround him, lapping waters not.
The chair, window, father have left but
still I think of ways I resemble him,
the ways I don't. I was never privy to his thoughts.
Alone, I am privy to my own.

Living with Mother

And this is how it once was.
I, replacing my father, sit at the window,
besieged by my mother's anxieties
about a ceiling falling, an incontinent cat,
and I will be blamed,
blamed if it happens, blamed
for the fear of its happening.
I will retreat to the cruelty of silence,
my face averted to the window
or take a walk, talking to myself,
or drink and drink and drink,
one moment stuporous, the other
recriminative. My mother,
anxious with her murderous headache,
lives on and on,
and I, my father's shell, await my end.

How Your Mother Dies

You pound and pound on the glass door.
The doorman takes his time.
It's a small-town hospital.
Your mother's transported by moans
in a wheelchair down a short hall
that is too long.
It's her heart.
The curt nurse sleepwalks.
On the table at last a mask,
a way your mother can breathe.
Another nurse arrives.
Your mother's body shudders
from the shocks.
A doctor roused from sleep miles away
shoos you from the room.
You wait.
The doorman tells you about his heart trouble.
They give you her clothes in a plastic bag.

III. LONGING

Max

the Welsh cob hired for
a little girl's summer riding
trots across the paddock,
grabs at my shirt.
That night he bolts over
the split rail fence,
makes tracks overland,
but is rounded up.
The consensus is he's lonely.

The fence repaired,
he stands at the far end
unmoving staring
into the middle distance of the woods.
Plainly, he's depressed.
Max reminds me of my past
seeking and finding women.
First I was lonely.
Then I was depressed.

After Cavafy

Leaving the party we walked
Toronto streets. Streetlamps on,
the moon was up, it was autumn,
we kicked at mounds of maple leaves.
She had long legs, an ugly friendly face
and said, "Isn't life wonderful?
Isn't life great?"
At her apartment we drank wine.
I didn't want to leave. We went to bed
but she was having her period.
She skilfully whacked me off
and I was grateful.
Next day with a tiny fluffy dog
she walked me to the subway.
I don't recall if I asked her for a date
or if I did whether she declined.
Although I never saw her again
I remember her.
I often wonder if she's married
and has six children
as I wonder about the others
who made me happy or unhappy.

Is There Love in Your Life?

— a friend's query

No, and then a stranger drifts across
your field, sent by a breeze
and it's high summer.
Though this person
has habits and problems as you do,
though the future that lies before you lies,
though you know this
though the intersection
spells trouble in triplicate
there is only the motion of her inclination, how
she leans this way, that.

Each encounter you notice
imperfect pieces randomly arrange
in shuffle and reassembly
and you know she knows you know this,
how the sweet moment sours
little by little, more and more,
yet you wait breathless for her hair
to brush against your shoulder, and with one hand

she puts it up
and that's all it is,
as both of you, conferring, wait for love to go away.

Through

Through the ways of seeing you
I find the fact within the act
your body makes for me,
through the I inside the my,
through sounds escaping bounds,
through your skin a skin within,
through your remit the way to it.
Through the lens of might-have-beens
I see the what-could-be,
through the loan of you what it is I own.
Through your being near, being here,
I count the cost of what I've lost.
You are everything that passes in your passing through.

IV. SCENES FROM DOMESTIC LIFE

When I Come in from the Cold

When I come in from the cold
gloveless, lugging bags of groceries
in frozen hands and yell, *"It's so fucking cold!"*
you assume that I'm accusing you of neglect
or blaming you, on general principles,
for everything. You could, but do not, yell,
"I can't do anything about the weather!"
or *"Why don't you buy some fucking gloves!"*
But nonetheless you too are yelling, furious,
the air still heated, my hands still cold.

My Wife Likes to Garden

Which is why she sits barefoot in the soil
of her flower garden,
neck-deep in greenness, like a rabbit in tall grass
sounding the air around herself
beside the red oak sapling, rusty already in June.
She may be tugging something from the earth,
an undesired plant. Or is it enough
to sit and feel this garden stir?
The garden in fact's a bit of a jungle,
her accommodation with the wild,
and she has madness in her method
admired by curious passers-by.
What's that? Is it an iris?
That mauve and white thing's Dame's rocket.
The garden grows up. Gathered, it gathers around her.
sprung from her hands.
And milkweed. Butterflies!
They're airborne. She's earthbound.

Watching My Wife Do Gardening

this unseasonably warm weekday in March
I am seized with an access of affection
at her spading and trowelling,
shifting and shuttling,
but don't know why.
What she does seems purposive but circular,
ends and means the same,
what she does and what results from it
unpredictable yet commendable.
My wife's companioned by her poodle
who scrabbles at soggy ground
near the compostor, rumoured to be
the dwelling place of rats,
his digging like hers
purposeful, perhaps ineffectual,
while in the next yard the chow on his long rope
rumbles back and forth,
shouting outrage or instruction.
Now my wife is hurrying to another corner,
tender and implacable.
From my upstairs window I look down
at this eventful commonplaceness,
reflecting that although I do not garden

Fraser Sutherland

it is good to have a garden
and someone in it.

My Wife Lies on the Grass

My wife is lying curled on the grass,
nothing beneath her but the weighted grass.
The way the smell of heated grease fills a room
she fills the backyard like a solo casualty
of a soon-to-be-forgotten war, the contained
and the container. Her mother apparently
never warned her this is how you catch
your death of cold. Despite the warm sun
the day is cool. Some time before
she'd stroked the orange cat beside her
until she was summoned by the earth.
How long will she lie there, all by herself?
I don't know, no more do I know why she
does anything she does, though always she emerges
with a reason. So there may be one in this case
should she wake.

V. SON

Lines for My Son

He is tiny, plump, and the room's light
doesn't come from beyond the ruby curtains,
it's generated by his grin,
his grip on the pen's slats,
A bright pillar in the smoke of our lives.

Like a fainter glow when his mother first shone
in bed's nightness to write my address,
an envelope's ballast of joy.

If with years waking corpuscles dim
where did they go except
to make this only son's mild torch?

Fall from a Castle

As he snapped the shutter he saw in the frame
his son of three years falling,
falling from a parapet.
He saw his son in empty space
suspended, the rocks below.
Crazily, he thought not of a crushed small body
but Icarus, a frame cunningly made,
He could not cry out that gravity relent,
cry out at all. He could not think
of rock, earth, clouds, or air. All was this
looking, a mouth open.

Alaska

And this is how it may for what remains of time. I will sit with my son in the locked waiting room of an emergency ward of a psychiatric hospital while inside a glass-walled paddock the staff wanders on undisclosed errands among their whiteboards, charts, and pigeonholes, or sit staring indifferently at their uninformative computer screens while outside it the waiting clients slump in somnolence or in various states of uncomplaining pissed-offedness while the seconds, minutes, and hours tick by and the television mounted above our heads silently reflects the latticed lights of the ceiling and the outdoor joys of scenic Alaska.

Remembering

"I don't want to forget him!"
his mother said.
As if remembering would bring him back,
as if thinking what he would say or do
could make him say and do.
But is it about him at all?
Is remembering only proof that we lived
with him during years, 26 of them?
Asking to remember only the good things,
laughter and delight ⊠ what kind of life was that?
Without the misery and craziness, a life half-lived.
A "celebration of the life..." That formula.
Thanks loads for having lived.
Suppose we do remember everything,
the joy and grief, the boredom and anxiety,
what room is left for us to live,
what's left for others to remember us?

Putting on a Suit

Putting on a suit
I thought of another year, another suit.
It was the day of my son's funeral
and I couldn't find my suit.
But there was another suit I found
that fitted me,
A dark blue suit very like my own.
His.

The Visitor

Another person arrived,
put into our keeping.
A stranger, yet he resembled us in part.
What he would become we didn't know,
he was all becoming,
not least the way he grew
apart from us. That part
came into its own.
We watched this stranger grow,
grow taller, make friends,
undergo glee and lovelost grief.
When he stopped growing
and wrapped himself in magic,
he was stranger still.
From what planet or underworld
had he come? The visitor
had no answers for us,
he was looking for his own.
He found them in a corner of his brain.
The trouble was, his trouble, our trouble,
they were voices accusing
him, and that he must atone,

perhaps for being who he was,
a visitor.

VI. STUDIES FROM HISTORY

In Time of War

> *And maps can really point to places*
> *Where life is evil now:*
> *Nanking; Dachau.*

W. H. Auden, "In Time of War"

The maps are different but
people suffer anyhow
where evil happens now.

On a far continent or down the street
bullets or bomb blasts endow
places where evil happens now.

The ordinary tragedies of life
might seem sufficient to not allow
for places where evil happens now.

1919

Stuttering frames, goose-stepping ghosts,
a Tourette's Syndrome parade,
smoke-trailing trains trapped in the spastic instant,
high-stepping landau horses on the Champs Elysées,
knee-jerk embraces, piebald crowds,
white-jowled statesmen in bowlers and top hats,
racewalking with skirt-hobbled women
hurriedly lost in the postwar century.
Shucking greatcoats, they will sit
under Hôtel Crillon chandeliers, among Versailles mirrors,
and piece a jigsaw puzzle of the continent.
What do capped workers think, hefting crates into corner
épiceries?
Something happening today? History?

Consistency

When the soldiers came in their armoured vehicle they gave the little Muslim boys candy bars. They gave pieces of candy bars to barking or tail-wagging dogs. When the soldiers drove away, some of the boys ran after them, ran and ran and ran until there was only one boy, running, running.

The next time the men came they taught the little boys to chant in English, "I love pork! I love pork!" Later, one of the soldiers seized a woolly black-and-white puppy waddling nearby. The puppy squealed in shock and the soldier hurled it in a great arc over a cliff. One of the grinning soldiers said, "Hey, that's *mean.*"

The local people hated the soldiers when they were kindly. They hated them when they were cruel. Mostly, they hated them because they were inconsistent.

Letter to Jim Jones

Some reduction is achievable
amid documentary impedimenta:
your voice, rant, rave.

Not that words often do good.
Not your words anyway.
To write about you makes us captive
like those who followed you.

You returned them to earth.
to jungle putrefaction.
They lay with you in the hacked space
you called a town
so all should rot and let us smell you.

Marines

The mind is a mischievous thing.
Why should I wake up with the U.S. Marines anthem on
the brain?
From the halls of Montezuma to the shores of Tripoli...

All the Marine NCOs and officers died
storming Chapultepec Castle near Mexico City
but California was won.

Ten Marines and Greek, Arab, and Berber mercenaries
flew the flag over Derne, port on the Barbary Coast,
though we're not sure what was won.
Nor were the mercenaries paid.

Blowhards, the Marines. But a fine body of fighting men.

Flying to Manhattan

Looped ribbons, frayed threads,
the glinting metal beads of habitation
as the plane slants at the end of June,
a taught arrow to its target.
The river widens to an ocean,
the plane sinks toward Moloch
shorn of twin heights
but still with its bench-sitters, its doorstep sitters.
Green amid grey or, nature in motion,
boys dunk shots through the high summer
of most and least America.
Soon the spangled starbursts.
It's mere days before the Fourth of July.

On Our Election

A pudding-face has been deposed
by a younger man with better abs.
Forget his plausible drone, his sullen snits,
the half-smiles that barely missed a yawn,
forget the closet wherein his men
quietly practised lying by omission,
forget his gassy make-public men.
Why did we put up with him so long?
We disliked him but got what we paid for,
tax credits for pogo sticks.
True, our ideals were often bullshit,
our dissidence he labelled not for export.
He picked one favourite contested country,
closed an embassy to another.
He took pride in his thick hide.
Consoled by suburbs, he wasn't in it for the spoils,
only power. For a politician what else could it be?
Let's not be hard on him.

VII. STUDIES FROM LIVES

Round

The engine throbs beneath him,
the turning of the screw.
If he turns the wheel enough
he'll make the grid come true.

He mows his neighbour's lawn,
their visitors arrive to stay.
His neighbour's guests don't care.
They tread on it anyway.

When the invaders leave
he waits until they're out of sight.
Then he mows it again,
purification rite.

Each extra inch of growth
is vulgar and obscene.
If he could, he'd paint the lawn
a different shade of green.
 The tractor's an expense, of course,
and, naturally, the cost of gas.

But, after all, such money spent
is nothing to the cost of grass

that, left alone, would grow and grow,
take over everything,
would swamp his tractor, house, and car,
one reason why he's mowing.

He numbers every blade of grass,
establishing its border.
His work is never done, alas,
the world is in disorder.

George McCready Price (1870-1963)

First Day New Brunswicker, Seventh Day Californian,
farmer, tract peddler, schoolmaster, construction teamster,
handyman Adventist evangelist, student of the rocks.
All his sincere toiling days he warred against
Genesis-denying tobacco-smoking Sabbath-breaking God
defiers
like Agassiz with his continent-sprawling ice sheets,
Darwin and his ape granddaddies. The Hun,
Darwinists to a man, brought us World War One.
Satan, the great hybridizer, spawned mixed-race degener-
ates.
Thank God the Last Days are imminent.

The Rocks! Yes, there are fossils in the rocks,
and columned strata beloved of evolutionists.
But wait! Early fossils lie atop late fossils,
a layer of Cambrian squats on the young Cretaceous.
Now why is that? Geologists assert thrust faults.
Common sense tells him they're detritus of the Flood,
the Noachian catastrophe. But fellow creation scientists
are fallible. They bother about how many eons came before
the Fall,
how much elbow room the Ark contained for pairs.

At 93, a Precambrian age, dies George McCready Price.
The Flood! The Flood has carried him off.

Neal Cassady

Rubbing his hurting belly, he's on the road to dig
mad mysterious strange holy crazy America
with a whoo-hee! Aw! Hup! Hup! Ah-hem! *Yes*! Yass, yass
in a roar, rush, race, and zoom he balls the jack
with cars he steals or drops off, new when he gets them,
beat when he's done with them,
and at the curb sweet gentle gur-ruls, who in coldwater
pads
will be new wives who give him new kids
and tell him to get out and he does
to find junkie coloured faggot hipster saints
in hornblow bop nights when he hits the bars
with kicks of weed and pills, hitches to hitchhikers,
improves himself with downtime Nietzsche talk,
humps hunnerdweight tires and shimmies cars into lot
spots
between searching for his tinsmith wino father
but what he'll do when he finds him
he doesn't know but in the meantime lessgo.

Thank You Speech

The tireless volunteer steps shyly forward to receive her
framed award.
Blinking in the light, she thanks first the master of ceremo-
nies
and the committee that chose her as this year's recipient.
She thanks everyone who's come here tonight and also her
husband Neil,
whom she deprived those long nights she stuffed enve-
lopes,
and her children Betty, Peter, and Todd, who were patient,
too.
The audience chuckles. She stresses the importance of vol-
untarism,
she urges that more people go out and get involved.
*Here and there among the darkened seats some nod appre-
ciatively.*
She observes what a privilege it's been to work with caring
people.

She asks that she be allowed to inject a personal note, how
growing up in a small town she learned how people can
contribute.
In her own family her father often said

you have to think of others once in a while, and her
mother
took an active role in her community's affairs.
The audience stirs slightly, this is going on a shade too long.
She and her brothers learned that lesson well, though
of course there is always more to do.
She remembers how her high school class was always
mounting drives,
selling magazine subscriptions and chocolate bars.

It's true that her school memories were not entirely happy,
that math teacher who offered extra tutoring
and then something happened too painful to recall
which is why she's taking the opportunity now
to remind everyone of the plight of children abused
by those with power, and if her own sufferings inspire
an honest examination of the past then what she went
through was not in vain.
Fair enough, but is this the time or place?

When she went to university she became exposed
to people from many other lands, and feels grateful
hey have shared their cultures, they have given much to
Canada
and perhaps this may be the time

to thank Lo Fong of Dang Ho Restaurant, who makes the best
shrimp on sugar cane in town, bar none, and Marcello,
stylist at Gianni's, because only he can solve her impossible hair!
A few people near the doors have begun to leave.

This morning after coffee she looked out at the back garden
where the lovely autumn leaves have fallen and thought,
"My goodness, I'm so lucky, we're all so lucky here."
At home there's been a bit of problem meeting the mortgage
and she wishes the government would do something in the way
of tax relief though not at the price of slashing our social services,
which is why she's always voted Liberal.
The departees have become a steady stream.

But this is no time to get into politics because
the world is changing and national borders no longer mean
what they did. If ethnic cleansing flourishes,
if evil thrives somewhere something must be done.
As John Donne said, "Never ask for whom the bell tolls,

it tolls for thee." *An uncertain murmur of approval,*
one or two people pause for a moment at the exits.
She thought of that this morning when the alarm went off
and found herself under only half a blanket.
She got to wondering whether natural fibres really
make any difference under these conditions.
Life consists of quieting fears and finding new ways to
move on.

Now the worried impresario
is thinking about maybe cutting off the sound, or
calling security. Empty seats gape
as the hall becomes depleted, the speaker no longer sees
her audience, there is only the microphone,
her eyes staring into space.

As a woman she came to realize that, unlike men, she
learned the language
of the body at an early age and to put no distance
between her skin and the world around it, which makes
her,
she knows, vulnerable. *The M.C. braves the stage,*
whispers into the speaker's ear. No! She will not be silenced!
This strikes a chord. A few sisters stand in solidarity.
Then they march forward to join her at the mike.

My God, she's totally forgotten
to thank their cat Poko, the calico one, and Gigi, the half-
Dalmatian, plucked from the animal shelter, who instantly
became part of the family. *The women exchange glances
and edge toward the wings.* After this is over, she, Neil, and
the kids
plan to celebrate by going to Dang Ho, hoping
it's Lo Fong's shift, or to Gianni's if it's open this late
so Marcello can fix her hair, which should have been done
this morning
though Marcello's been ill lately, something about over-
work.

This morning driving to her job
some squeegee kids swarmed her car, and one of them
rode her hood all the way down to underground parking.
They made passionate love behind a Honda Civic and
does anyone here think twice about how office plants feel?
How many realize a hundred thousand glands sweat in the
average human foot
or that one ordinary human sneeze can infect Lake
Ontario?
Does anyone even stop to think about this kind of thing?
She thinks about it, more or less all the time.
*The hall's now empty, even the fascinated appalled have left,
even her*

beaming husband and proud children have vanished. The
lights are quenched,
the microphone dead, there is only her voice in the void.
Thank you very much.

Malvolio in a Good Mood

But not for long. Though he runs the household well
he's primed for a fall. So he's made to misconstrue
the lines of the prankish forged letter,
imagines that Olivia's writing them.
He is pompous and self-important, yes,
but this is not the ultimate offence.
It's that he dares to presume. A climber himself,
Shakespeare never lets go by the chance
to saw a rung from a social ladder,
to kick in the slats someone who presumes to rise.
Yet, being Shakespeare, he cannot help giving
his yellow cross-gartered dupe
the best role in the whole cross-dressing play.
The steward makes a fool of himself,
pitching woo to Olivia. Such effrontery!
But Malvolio, consigned to a madman's cell,
conducts a treasure hunt for dignity in tears.
Olivia's sorry for him but no one else is.
Shakespeare sorts out busy transvestite confusion
for a happy-ever-after. As for Malvolio,
he utters the stage villain's tired timeless cry:
"I'll be revenged on the whole pack of you."

The crickets will rub along as best they can
and soon the place will be up for sale.

Leaving

Since I heard about it, I've been talking to myself,
trying to explain why she left a marriage
of 30 years, a husband I knew as long.
I'd taken them for granted, people who had settled in.
Without warning, or none we saw, she left a note.
She left a note and flew to another continent
with a change of clothes. Their marriage contained
contrasting temperaments, thus stronger we believed.
If taking for granted was our case, we're now disabused.
If God is the inexplicable, we're believers now.

I think of the aged Tolstoy who fled his wife,
or the wife in a Bergman film who tells the camera
all her life she'd not been loved.
We look to find the fault in split rock.
Had she entered the breathing shade of the poet
to whose coastal shrine she was a pilgrim?
Was she invited into someone's churning dance?
She'd seemed averse to romance of any kind.
She summed her marriage up and found it wanting.
To seize the moment abolishes all foregoing.
Something took to pieces what she and he had made.

Fatal Attraction

The plot: midmarried lawyer gets bit on the side.
Turns out she's a psycho.
She incinerates his car, does other things
even more worrying.
But how much more interesting's
the nightmare she leads him to
than his happy dishrag of a wife,
their small angelic boy.
Past men shouldering carcasses
the harpy, Medusa-curled, ascends
with him in a cage.
Ever done it in a freight elevator?
No, he hasn't. Inside her cave,
her buttocks ridged on the kitchen sink,
he thrusts and she reaches back
to splash water on her breasts,
his face cools and heats.
At the weekend's close she slashes her wrists.
Her dementia's tirelessly inventive,
likewise her despair. While Wife
cheerfully rolls paint on the ceiling
of a newbought home
Other Woman sinks into *Madame Butterfly's*

soaring aria, switches the light
on and off, off and on.
All these are good ideas.
It means she takes things seriously.

Mrs. Robinson

It was not your fault the conjunction
of Triple A track star
and husband-jackass told you
there wasn't much time left.

You hitched a delectable nyloned thigh
for a cuddly, fleet-footed graduate.
"Mrs. Robinson.... you're trying to seduce me!"
It was, perhaps, your best moment.

But time tracked you
and you ran through muddying rain,
the good lines smudged,
your hair a mess, make-up erased.

Then the track star ran off with your daughter.
They fled aboard a crowded bus.
Miss Robinson may become Mrs. Robinson,
the track star's beaten by a new comer.
 Did you marry badly, Mrs. Robinson?
You only wanted what everyone else did.
There was freedom in tumbled sheets.
For the time being there was nowhere else to go.

Pascale

Pascale Ogier, dead on the day before her twenty-fifth birthday, in the same year her last film was released, Eric Rohmer's *Les Nuits de la pleine lune,* retitled *Full Moon in Paris* for Anglophone consumption. Dead of a drug overdose, complicated by the heart murmur she'd had half her life, or vice versa.

Here is she walking in the greyness of the winter months, a woolly wrap cloaking her ethereal, though not ephemeral, figure. On one occasion we see her tiny perfect boobs and bum, too vulgar put so, and breasts and buttocks, too formal and stilted put so. Always we see the enormous eyes and the mood-shifting triangular face, mirroring the emotive triangle in which she is implicated, a plane figure that expands into a problematic quadrilateral.

Louise lives in the Paris suburb of Marne-la-Valée with Rémy, a new-town architect who is tortured by her propensity to stay out late at night. A tennis player, stolid, he is not one for late nights. She works in the centre of Paris as an interior decorator trainee, with a sideline in lamp-making, as if it might shed illumination on her confusion.

She decides she needs a little apartment, a pied-à-terre to fulfil what may be her destiny as a party girl or perhaps, as she says at one point, to learn loneliness. A potted summary of the film says she "wants to have it all," which is not correct. Neither is it correct to say she wants her freedom, or even a room of her own. Rohmer and we want her to be what she is.

In Paris she is doggedly pursued by Octave, who is married. He is intelligent, as most of Rohmer's people are, and hapless, as some of them are. He desires her body, but she does not desire his. She wants him to be her friend. The role is played by Fabrice Luchini, who is Perceval le Gallois in another Rohmer film. Like Perceval, Octave is on a quest.

Louise's desire finds expression at a party in a full-contact dance with a Caliban, a sex sax player, the bestial Bastien. Later she lies on her side of the bed while the beast sleeps on. Her enormous eyes stare into dimness.

She trudges at dawn out to Marne-la-Valée, hoping to find Rémy. He isn't there. When he returns, she learns that he has found another woman, maybe steadier. She phones Octave, the no-hoper, to arrange a meeting the next day. Outside, she plods toward a No Exit sign.

Les Nuits… belongs to the series *Comédies et Proverbes*. In this case the "country proverb" Rohmer wrote himself. "He who has two women loses his soul. He who has two houses loses his mind." The he is she.

Rohmer's way is to mutually transform them. Pascale Ogier gets a design credit for the film. Rohmer surely could not have imagined that she would destroy her self-creation. Like Rohmer's name, hers was not the one to which she was attached at birth.

I take her death as a personal affront. She is the most beautiful woman I have ever seen on a screen. How dare she destroy herself? What right had she to go away?

VII. EDWARD

Traveller

All he does is eat, drink, chase shoeshine boys,
frustrated
at not living long enough
to have all of them.
Literature is a fad,

masturbatory unserious.
He's found where day and night converge,
lapsing into childhood,
witness to black and blue
and a jailhouse bunk.

He is in fact a child
whose milk has curdled.
He finds in brazen arms
the graven image of too many years.
His shrilling mother's dead.

The trouble with mothers
too much flesh
bringing you back.

His aunts the nuns are dying.
Extremes of warmth and cold.

Was the judge who sentenced Timothy Leary
and sentenced him the
bottled-hummingbird father
forever saying no?
Did they come from the same town?

His face to the sun,
he loses them.
The sun is a man.
Sometimes in the fluid night
he is submerged.

His mania is lists
but he never adds them up.
He likes roe, eggplant, pomegranate,
many-seeded liquid sex.
He loves and hates his path of snow.

He slides across the eyelid of a lover,
sweat shimmer to the Brownian movement
of bright day, the beach boys

of Copacabana. They exploit
and are exploited.

I suppose he finds the heart of the rose
in a boy's tattoo.
Determined fingers climb
the muscle diatonic,
the scales of touch.

I have looked for him
and go on looking,
a bar in Delhi,
or Rio de Janeiro.
They know him in all the embassies.

His hotels wander,
his letters circumnavigate,
and the desk-clerk says, oh
yes, he was here
but now he's gone.

The train waits but
he's further down the line.
He stays ahead of the plane he's on.

Shedding books and clothes, he travels light
riding the molecules of dusty skins.

He may be many things,
the dolphin of the boy bars,
a cruising shark.
His smoked glasses
reflect ice.

Some day he'll join us,
the many and the one,
row on row of us,
and the last dead man
it will be him.

For E.A.L.

This is your country,
Canada hater,
as much as you fight it
it will follow.

The snow that froze you out,
froze you to the bone,
is always with you,
vehemently validating

your skin's transparency
to the plural, to heat,
to light, the quick
tingling as you walk

the far roads oceanic.
Wherever you are,
you think of us here.

The Year of Living Dangerously

Edward, I am reading the tattered paperback
among effects you left behind,
about a reporter and his dwarf cameraman
in Sukarno's Jakarta.
The Year of Living Dangerously.
It was with you in that Jakarta teaching job.
You abandoned it, though not this book
reeking of piss, sweat, and pong.
It went with you through the ovens of Southeast Asia,
speaks of dangling light-bulb rooms,
of bars and boys.
After the speeding Bangkok motorist broke your head
and dumped you at a hospital
it was with you on the long flight home.
Crammed in a vinyl suitcase it kept company
with seashells, ragged manuscripts.
Shunted from one institution to another
it came to rest in my cool dark basement.
Now I turn each dried sodden page
that speaks of panic, booze, and fear.
As it happens, Edward,
this is my own year of living dangerously
though not as dangerously as you.

Edward Street

is where they scraped you off the pavement
trucking you to some cool floor
where out of patience and purse-strings
they dump you
because even your best friends
will not join you in the street.
What did you on the street?
You walked, got to the end,
turned back, each street different,
each the same but now
the legs that have taken
the street to the ends of the world
will no longer carry you.
Living is what someone else must do for you.
The street contracts.
It's after all a short street,
a dead end from which you cannot turn,
not that you ever heeded signals,
wards, or wardens,
not that you ever wanted to leave
the street. You the always-self-determined,
ever-passive, this is your street.
Edward Street.

Father and Son

A banal incident of parenting.
In the parking lot of a pizza house
off a main street heading out of town
a father's furious. "Get in the car!" he yells
at his son. It's about 6 p.m.,
cloudy, night gathering. Beyond the boy
his friend looks equally unhappy.
They're both in baggy teenage uniform.
It's the son's face you observe, he's in trouble,
his face caving inward.
Take close notice of his collapsing face.
Soon it will harden into something unrecognizable.

Lindsay, Ontario

XIX. ENVIRONS

Encampments

The day starts from the ground up,
faces flesh out themselves.
Steps lead into a corner church.
On them one, two, three winos
watch the thudding, thumping
streetcars westbound.

These men swig from paperbagged tiny bottles
of bitters bought in convenience stores.
A lost fair lady stops her car, they hurry to her.
Gracious, she nods and makes a swift U-turn.
They return to dank cement, sit
hands splayed, palms open
as for a soul rap or stigmata
in the shadow of the risen Lord.

One shuffles and staggers across the sunburnt lawn,
a bummed cigarette crosses back and forth.
Other arrangements are possible.
A jumble of broken chairs semi-circular
beneath a junior maple. Across

the street a body's tightly coiled
behind a hedge, curled up in a carpet.

Unless the castle was under siege
grizzled peasants made crude habitation
in lean-to huddled huts. They
crouched around damp wood fires whose smoke
rose to the tower, told the prince
these also were his subjects.

Walls are ivy-bannered, bricks
baked dull or bright rose,
framed by dour putty.
In metal eaves, pigeons peck, daubing
shingled gables. On the steeple's copper lid
a seagull squats. The cross-hatched
ogival windows are opaque.

The pace quickens: pedestrians
sidewalk side-glance.
Only petunias are in flower.
The mendicants do not, just now, ask for alms.
Ravages of darkness must be reconstructed.

When the lord and his attendant lieges
quit the castle with harness jingle, clop of hooves
those who made encampment watched
long-shirted, in coarse wool leggings.

Although the prince ignored
their stooped, bent, bowed irrelevance

as he stalked forth to the work of war
these unlovely still had hope of crumbs.

Fraser Sutherland

Catholic Family at a Funeral

They are sad as they process down the aisle
at the close. It is, after all, a funeral.
They mourn him, father and grandfather
who raised them in the family of Christ.
The Latin mass, sung by special permission,
tells us that, though he had no merit,
he might still, by grace, enter the gates of heaven.
He was a good man: gentle, holy, and resolute.
He had a good death while his spouse,
who'd brought him to the faith, went on
dissolving in Alzheimer's at another place.
His children tread with their children
of assorted ages, a baby in a basket.
They look submissive and fettered
as if, long ago, they had surrendered.
Though secular tides batter the church's walls
they obey. Against legions who oppose, or worse,
ignore, theirs is a lonely road. The rest of us wait
until they have passed into the cold day of interment
and do their best to be fruitful, and multiply.

Fall of a Church

In a district of shops opening and closing,
unfolding and folding, was a church.
On the main floor were Filipino Baptists,
in the basement the affiliate Neighbourhood
made glad sounds unto the Lord up and down
from metal chairs. The church steps were
the seat where rubbies sat or slept.

On the steeple a gull glanced south to the lake,
pigeons whirred into the ivy, grey flutter
against the plaster-nubbled dun-red bricks.
Sparrows cross-hopped, squirrels darted,
chestnuts in cheek among turning maple branches.
Prostitutes were also active, patrolling the corner.
Cars stopped and started, life continued in this way

The Baptist Convention found maintenance too high.
The Filipinos left and the Neighbourhood
moved to a storefront. The church was rented.
Black women in flowing white gowns,
pastel turbans, marched under banners at 6 a.m.
crooning, "We are coming from the mountains
we are coming from the sea, we

are coming from JERUSALEM."
A sign appeared: *COLDWELL BANKER*
Retail Shops for Rent. A phone number. The man
in the office chuckled, "Demolition on the old church
will start shortly if it doesn't fall down by itself.
There'll be a little shopping plaza there by March."

The first machine arrived, men took soil samples
and trucked away the pews. A bearded man in shorts,
one of the crazed, ripped down the sign,
but could not uproot the metal stakes. A workman propped
a sign against the iron fence.
The ogival windows went first, turned into slots.
A dumpster squatted in back.
On hoardings posters for Tai Chi, Aquarium Fantasy.
Staple-gunners told us who to elect to city council.
Inside the church stacks of lath and kindling,

the blonde, brown-trimmed walls, cross-section
of a staircase. Whether the hard-hats with push-brooms
and crowbars were ants or termites could not be guessed.
In either case, it was surprising how quietly they worked.
At an early hour two or three leaned at the corner,
waiting for the boss. Someone else's spray-can wrote

WILL A MAN ROB GOD?
Bricks were disassembled, laths splintered.

Cars with stickers were allowed to park
and at rush-hour Friday night
the Caterpillar slid off the haulage truck,
triceps and claw dangling from a chain.
The claw scooped away the chancel, the entrance
shook. Plaster crumbled, clouds
winnowed in the street, a hose kept down the dust
as if putting out a fire.
Beyond the crawling machine a man in miniature
perched at the apex of a roof,
seated on a grid of boards, prying at a shingle.
Treads trampled corrugated piles of bricks,
sloped into the basement.

The scoop dug and dug.
Some days nothing happened,
not even wind circulated in the aisles.
Men in tartan jackets wandered the new field.
Twisted metal beams, incisor-gripped, edged off
the peaks. A rainfall of bricks that rose in mounds.
The claw dipped in prayer, cuddled walls.

Through window gaps shadows moved.
Gone were shingles, the slant of beams.
A bulldozer levelled the earth.

Boards were bundled. People strolled
among the bricks, taking away the tidiest.
Then the Hercules crane arrived to chew
away the steeple. Policemen directed traffic
as it toppled piece by piece. People lined the street.
It began to rain. With a movement almost delicate
walls were nudged down slab by slab.

Roof and steeple, copper-tipped, were rubble.
By February the bulldozer
cuddled the last hill of bricks. On muddy roads
a white trailer stood.
People took away the wood, some
to grace antique shop interiors,
framing shards of glass. Meanwhile

more posters, a new dispensation.
Here was Elizabeth Claire Prophet
teaching the ASCENDED MASTERS
MESSENGER FOR THE GREAT BROTHERHOOD.

Another soul spray-painted
CURSED BE THE MAN WHO CURSES MY LORD.
Beyond the boards, even girders were gone.

The tilled field harvested snow.
On a shallow foundation
a low shell crouched, faced by window cardboard signs
Then customers caught short or curious
began to buy whatever was for sale.

There were no squirrels, birds,
rubbies, no prostitutes, and no church.

Panhandler

When, drug-addled, on the street, he hits you up
for a quarter, a dollar, a million dollars,
or just a cigarette and a light he can take nearby
to a hunched huddled figure,
his care for it cuts you with a jagged wound.
He has a story. You could hear his story
if you had time to listen,
you could tell him your story
but he also has no time to listen,
he's too busy begging.
Not that your story is better shaped,
more glamorously sordid,
You just don't think that the telling
will bring release and relief to him or you.
Anyway, it's flinging money down a hole.
Nor, though your plight is less,
can you help him. Nor can he help you.

At the Cottage

Compass bearing north to the holy site, a cross between wilderness and suburbia.

The difficulties. The water pump needs daily delicate adjustments. The indoor toilet supplemented by the outdoor privy trekked to on bare feet on a pine-needled path. Electrical and electronic signals fading in and out. Piquant suggestion of pioneering and the struggle for survival.

To get there: main highway, secondary highway, private road to the marina, a water taxi dodging among stony islets, down aquatic avenues lined with rich men's palisades, slowing in shallows, then busting through deep water until a wake washes them up on a peopled shore, unloading at a weathered dock. The cottage on its granite perch squats among boulders. Out on the lake the loons do their gurgling whoops, swallowing eons of evolution.

What's remembered: not clear blue days sun lake but flat heaviness of sky and water merging. The monochrome may lift. On this corner of the bay, the slow slap of waves on rocks, somewhere out there muted cries and motions.

Fraser Sutherland

The Loon

The loon sits on a lake.
He is a black rock bobbing on blue ripples.
He stares quick at any shore.
He is analytical and ministerial.
He is keen-eyed and bored.
After a time he tucks into himself and disappears,
then surfaces a foot or half a mile from where he was.
At that moment he gargles with a fish
and resumes his role as a bobbing rock.
Now and then he calls that he's fed up with everything,
the shape of clouds, the quality of fish,
the ratio of lake to feathers.
He's fed up, he's fed up, he tells you.

Tropical Fish

There they go, flitting and gliding
in the big glass tank above the bar.
Now and then one nips the other on the tail
but generally they seem acqueously content
in shades of gold, angel, and *éminence grise,*

and what about the multidoored floating chalices of
streetcars
and, seen through their windows, me.

Our Neighbours Are Moving

Our next door neighbours, the Silvers, are moving.
They're not dead, they're moving.
Hi-ho, Silvers, away!
Though the house was sold months ago, it happens quicksilver,
a moving van at the curb, side doors wide open
to receive their worldly goods except their two small boys,
take them across a continent. The yard toys go in
but not the sandbox. The mattresses. The beds go last.
One of the movers shows Mrs. Silver the van's interior,
a temporary house. It is satisfactory.
No one that I notice counts the silver.
Presence will become absence, ghosts with nothing to say.
New occupants will move in, perhaps the Golds.

XX. ELEMENTS

AIR

We hardly ever notice the mixture of gases that surround us. We only realize it if there is a strong wind or when fog or smog cuts off our view. Yet we depend on air in many ways.
    "Science Encyclopedia," *The New Lexicon Webster's Dictionary of the English Language*

It seems to be free but isn't, this element in which we
move.
When a bird soars it seems to disappear inside itself
but that speck diminishing has lost and gained so much
it seems to be nothing, or else is everything.
When we kick a ball we push against something else,
exertion, pressure, force, torque, or thrust.
But the moment this is done, little remains
except some memory of striking, a trace of violence
that happened once in what is now denatured, thus
we hardly ever notice the mixture of gases that surround
us.

But is that true? The glossy perfume ad
reeks that we've given air something to think about
but smelling the new reality we know we've taken

what once was freely given, and in its stead,
replaced it with odoriferous alternatives,
that we've made ourselves a din
in the decorous silences of day.
Our labs and dollars thicken the atmosphere
so there's nothing left but us, not what we rescind.
We only realize it if there is a strong wind,

reminding us of what's beyond, the wildness
of what we can't control, that gangs up on us
as tornado, cyclone, hurricane. So we fake it
with the air conditioner, a synthetic breeze,
a blowing substitute for what we fear,
indoor recirculation inducing what is owed
we feel, to us. Now step to the window.
We're reminded suddenly it's after all still there,
it's there in drifts remaining from what blew
or when fog or smog cuts off our view.

Perhaps we'll avoid all this, build a machine
that does the breathing for us, another to offer
climatic variety. Then the air will be
wholly ours to buy, sell, conserve, or spend.
We'll hug it to ourselves, a portable lung.

But who or what makes the stuff? Who rules
it's our inheritance or right, or that
it's wholly contained within our scope?

We ignore it during all the makeshift days
yet we depend on air in many ways.

Dust

The dust that spots the edge of books like a skin disease,
that sits on the Saharan floor of shelves,
that talcs the web of spiders in dry seasons, their only
seasons,
that layers basements with a subtle erosion,
the dust that powders china cups and plates,
recalling them to their elements.
The dust that rides all winter the interior of cottages,
that drifts across the sun roofs of sleeping cars
while other cars on country roads say, "Eat my dust!"
The slow slight sediment on lenses
that settles, an incurable curtain on the visible,
that adds floating seams in coal-mine corridors,
that awaits sparrows to kick up dust,
the dust that augments a rubber plant
and doubles the leaves of our pages
shaken awake with the gust of our breath.
The dust the wind turns into dunes.

XIII. CHINA

China

Standing by pillars of palms in the muggy night,
millions of people downslope from me, I cultivate
my habit of, and talent for, unhappiness,
fretting at familiar unquiet nittinesses, still drinking
the portable unpotable water of neuroses,
the palms' shed rattling leaves making no difference,
nor women in blue sweeping them, nor scalloped roofs,
nor woofing frogs or wobbling carp in the little river,
nor unstirring steambath, unshaded furnace blast,
nor skin lemony, coppery, aged ivory,
nor tones that go down, up, level, go up and down.
Brooding whether I can ever hive off
the irritated shell that houses me.
Can this possibly be where longing meets belonging?
You are here. Expect nothing more. This is China.

Spring on Guangwai Campus, Guangzhou

A lean old man has had his eye on a tree,
he cranes a pole device like a fishing rod
to snip or snag a bud or bug from a jointed branch.
Beneath clumped waterplants in the little river
comes two-note frogsound like a chugging rasping file.
Trees rain flowers like flame-coloured expansive tulips.
Women and men pick them up and turn them in their
hands.
Small boys pick them up as well
and in the sandy margin of their playing field
dig a big hole and reverently bury them.

The Dim Sum Ballroom

Past dawn they ramble into the Dim Sum Ballroom,
the Codgers Club, at ease in well-worn eccentricity.
I have grown fond of them, how
they rally saucer, cup, bowl, chopsticks, teapot,
plod to canisters of tea, spigots of scalding water.
They rinse their dishes with cleansing tea
and dump it in a plastic bowl on the lazy susan,
at the steam table point at dumplings.
Jacketed youths, glazed by early rising,
plunk choices on trays, rubber-stamp the bills.
A woman comes round to toss toothpicks on the tables.
The codgers pluck at steamed buns and from soup
spit out bony bits. A codger here and there swigs
brandy or goes about a postprandial smoke.
My eyes take them in, all of them, my skin,
alarmingly white in the brown-yellow weave,
begs admission to the company of codgers
and with them start the day. In a year
a few of them may not be around, no more may I.
Yet while we're here we can share
what life gives us in its small amounts.

Whiteness

There is the whiteness of the horse or the whiteness of the snow in ancient Chinese philosophy, but not whiteness as an abstract, detachable concept that can be applied to almost anything.
    Richard E. Nisbett, *The Geography of Thought: How Asians and Westerners Think Differently... and why*

    The white of a polar bear that fails to do its laundry,
    the white of the snow where the polar bear pees —
    but that wouldn't be whiteness, would it?
    The white of the ice on which the polar bear walks,
    so pale it's nearly no colour —but that's what white is,
    isn't it? The white of a horse the polar bear meets.
    They startle one another with their whiteness.
    "What are *you* doing here?" they ask one another,
    each in his own white.

Ethnic Minorities

You can find them stripping kernels from dried cobs
swinging and whirling their wild hair,
they who conquered half the world.
Their hieroglyphics explain how it happened.
To think they lived on stilts, these people,
while braziers warmed their platform beds,
grandmothers made wine in vast crocks
and bare feet spun a waterwheel.
Far from knowing who and where we were
they lived in forest hutments,
tuning their long-necked instruments
and worshipped just about anything.
How the days passed only they could tell.

Massage

I did not come to Hong Kong for a massage
but it's hard to convince otherwise
the thickly made-up woman keeping long hours
in the doorway of the building in which
my pillbox windowless room resides.
Why would anyone want a massage
even to keep out of the rain pouring which it's been doing
all afternoon as the woman pursues her thankless task
of handing out her invitations. A younger associate
urges me to get a massage and I refuse
once more as the rain keeps streaming.
She asks me where I'm from and I say "Canada,"
She says lots of Americans want massages
but she doesn't know about Canada. People advance
into the building and maybe they're going to their rooms
or maybe to offices or the premises of a bespoke tailor
whose sales force is out on the street dodging the down-
pour
and it's the kind of day one has to ask why anybody
would want to come to Hong Kong for a massage
or for any reason at all. Yet many do.

Guangzhou College Girl Prepares for a Class

A miniature in white T-shirt and pony tail,
she paces in the sun, one hand sheathing papers,
the other with Javanese gestures silently declaiming.
This is a university of foreign studies
so she speaks in a foreign language,
perhaps telling of rainforest burial customs,
how China's Gross Domestic Product relates to the euro,
that Ophelia explains to the Prince why the weather
tomorrow
will be the same steam it is today.
Her recitation is graceful, predetermined,
and if her classroom lacks the space of this cemented quad
her actual delivery may count for more.
She glances at a top sheet now and then,
a memory aid maybe, though it may also be
part of her presentation. She moves smoothly on
in rehearsal, audition, declaration.
One wrist lifts, one falls, fingers close, a palm opens,
disclosing all she offers to the empty air.

Companionship

Guangzhou, China

A friend saw two women
squatting by the road,
companionably chatting
and taking a dump.

He tried to ignore them,
knowing if he didn't, they'd say,
"What are *you* looking at?"

Why do anything alone
when you can do it together?

Enough

If you have enough people anything can happen.
Everything can happen if you have enough people.
If something uniquely good happens it's called a miracle
but it can't happen if there aren't many people it can happen to.
When something uniquely bad happens it calls for company
and gets it since there are so many who take it as their own.
For every catastrophe there's much more not happening
to most people because there are so many.
There are so many people, many just like you,
also just unlike you. You think you have a choice
but choice supposes just a few.
There are so many men, women, children
that any one growing up can be ideal for anyone.
Many go one way and many go another
because they all can't go the same way.
They can't because there are so many.
Anything can happen if you have enough people.

XXII. WHY AM I ME?

Angel

So many times it let you dodge the bullet.
So many times it saved your butt—
times deadfalls became pratfalls,
times you were an inch from death,
a micron from paralysis.
You could believe it was the hand of providence,
a promise of what would happen next,
an adventure in misadventure—
even madness was a form of reason.
Then the night comes when it
raises you from sleep,
gently takes you by the elbow
and flings you headlong down a flight of stairs.

Montaigne

We can live as long as we please, Montaigne says, but it won't reduce by the slightest
 the amount of time we're going to spend being dead.
  Philip Marchand in a book review, paraphrasing Michel de Montaigne

When you lose a son and say something about him
people shy away. It's to admit an unfortunate topic,
verges on bad taste, embarrasses them.
They don't know what to say or how to say it,
since any response they make will be inadequate,
remind them of the losses they will suffer.
Montaigne would have us think about it
more or less all the time, make it a pal,
part of a conversation with ourselves.
We should look forward calmly to the chance certainty.
Any pinprick, after all, could be an ending.
Every day, a favour, should be unexpected
as we plant cabbages, ever ready to go.
Such thoughts will help prepare us for our long career.

If, Like Me, You

If, like me, you sometimes think that a life's a cosmic joke
you must wonder at the joker's sense of fun
and what he gets from sportive diversions,
extended punch lines,
assuming there is a joker,
assuming he has this hobby.
Anyway, you were that comic favourite,
someone who takes himself seriously.
Naturally the banana peel you drop
is the one on which you trip.
It's implicit that your means acquire your ends
and that you end when you're sure you've just begun.
Your birth-cry was a howl of laughter,
your death-rattle will be a smattering of applause.
There are some things too funny to be borne
and some jokes carried way too far. To be a comic butt
may seem a fate you don't deserve. But it satisfies a need.

Laws

God gives laws like elephants and little green apples.
They lumber toward us with their swaying bulk, the elephants
trampling desires, setting fines for getting in the way.
The little green apples are round and hard sour spurting
in the mouth and the elephants dip their trunks for them,
eating their substance, eating their laws.
Laws are just a lot more stuff settling on the earth,
droppings of the elephant, undigested apples to punish our appetites,
more complex laws than a cat enforcing its code on a squirrel
or a tropical storm out at sea turning into a hurricane.
God gives laws but God is not law, and God bless God for that.

The Meonic

Three principles are active in the world: Providence, i.e. the super-cosmic God; freedom, i.e., the human spirit; and fate or destiny, i.e., Nature, the solidified, hardened outcome of the dark meonic freedom.
  Nicholas Berdyaev, *The Destiny of Man*

In the meonic you are free to choose
but there is nothing not to choose.
Being is one thing, non-being is not another.
There is no me in the meonic,
no sonic, no moronic, no Masonic.
None of the senses make sense here.
To say that it is no thing
is not to say that it is some thing.
God did not make it nor did it make God,
it is prior and has no public.
There is no there, only the only.
In the meonic you are free to do
but there is nothing to do and you are no longer you.
You cannot take something from the meonic.
It is, however, good prep when all is choice
and there is nothing to choose.
It is the dark matter of choice.

The Meonic cooked itself into a big batch of sludge.
This dark freedom hides within, a tumour of createdness.

Forgive God

Forgive God, the boundless fool, His blunders.
He made us in His image, forgive Him for it.
Forgive God for listening to prayers across trackless space
to the me, me, me, then absenting Himself to take a piss.
Forgive Him for not understanding,
or confusing us with too much understanding.
Forgive, take pity on Him alone in his Heaven
as though He cannot do without us.
Forgive God this muddled alibi for love.
Forgive God the excuses we make for him,
since forgive is stronger than excuse.
Forgive God the luxury of unbelief,
as if it matters whether we believe or not,
for making us think can improve the world,
for tilting us toward perfection
always ahead of us like a vanishing trail.
Forgive God for starting the fiery ball rolling
and His irresistible attraction to randomness,
his odd way of telling time.
Forgive God His indolence, so much to do
and too much time to do it in, a long-term lease
on the universe. Forgive God His mundane insults:
cancer, Alzheimer's, dementia. Forgive Him

for naming diseases after doctors.
Forgive Him nature's bad Darwin impersonations.
Forgive earthquakes, typhoons, tsunamis, tsetse flies,
all the flukes of His botched plan.
Forgive the Meccano blocks of name and shame
we impose as substitutes for Him.
Forgive God obtuseness paired with obliviousness,
Forgive Him His errors of subtraction and addition.
Forgive God. Just forgive.

Fraser Sutherland

Why Am I Me?

—title of a children's book

Good question: the me-ness of me.
You might also ask: why are you, you?
There's no point in asking when you were me.
It never happened.

Was it me from the start?
Did I begin with a glint in my mother's or father's eye?
Did it take nine months to be me?
And looking up and ahead and around

was it then I began to be me?
I was not alone. There was you.

AUTHOR BIO

Fraser Sutherland occupies a unique place in the literary culture of Canada. He is widely travelled, and has been a freelance writer, reporter and staff writer for major newspapers and magazines, including the *Toronto Star, Globe and Mail, Wall Street Journal, Quill & Quire,* and *Books in Canada.* He is widely admired as a critic and editor. He is the only Canadian poet who can claim to be a lexicographer having written and edited for dictionaries in three countries. He has published fourteen books in many genres ranging from poetry to history, business to essays, short story collections to a thesaurus. His work has been published in many journals and anthologies, and has been translated into Farsi, French, Italian, Albanian, and Serbo-Croat.